SELF-DISCIPLINE

*Develop Daily Habits to Program Your Mind and Build
Mental Toughness, Self-Confidence, and Willpower*

RAY VADEN

🏵 Created with Vellum

INTRODUCTION

In *Self-Discipline: Develop Daily Habits to Program Your Mind and Build Mental Toughness, Self-Confidence, and Willpower*, Ray Vaden will show how it is possible to develop a workable plan to reach the ultimate goal of self-discipline. Self-discipline goes by many names—self-control, sense of self-worth, and self-drive. They all point to the same fact: this person is in charge of themselves and knows how to utilize their inner strengths to get what they want out of life.

Many people wonder why self-discipline is so important. They wonder why they cannot just go on as they have been going on all this time, whirling around in their merry little unorganized lives. They can—if they so choose. Self-discipline is not mandatory. It is not something that is graded and measured such as the mortgage paid and what score was achieved on the driving test. Self-discipline is a purely internal force, and whether people have it and use it or not is a purely personal decision.

However, take a moment to consider a world without personal self-discipline. Think about what that might look like. In this world, no one has self-discipline. No one worries about getting anything finished in a timely manner. There are no priorities. There are no goals. Everyone just wanders through life happy and ignorant, choosing to ignore the fact that a better world might exist somewhere. This happy life is all well and good until the lights go out because the power was shut off because someone did not pay the power bill.

Now, imagine the same world where everyone has a sense of self-discipline. Of course, some people will be more highly developed than others—and that is okay—because everyone develops self-discipline at their own personal rate. Now, in this world, order and organization reign supreme. Bad habits are at a minimum. Good habits abound like happy little snowflakes floating everywhere. People are successful. Work gets done. The power bill gets paid, so no one is eating dinner in the dark.

Maybe that was embellished a bit, but it does paint a compelling picture. Life is so much better when the people running it possess a good sense of self-discipline. Self-control and self-discipline give humans the power to do anything they want to do. People with self-discipline are more successful at work because they are able to do more work in less time and really impress their bosses. Self-employed people with good self-discipline are able to take regular days off work to enjoy life because they, too, get more work done in less time. Now, they are impressing their families. In life, people with self-discipline are generally healthier because they know what needs to be done in order to replace bad habits with good ones. They also know ways to avoid starting a bad habit in the first place. Moreover, in relationships, people with self-discipline usually enjoy a deeper, more rewarding companionship because they know how to take care of themselves and others and how not to fall into petty little relationship-breaking traps.

By showing us ways to develop useful daily habits, this book will teach us that the goal of self-discipline is not only reachable but desirable as well. From learning to create a plan to acknowledging reality in our lives—all the way though enjoying the rewards that come with self-discipline—every necessary step will be outlined in easy-to-follow details. Mr. Vaden's hope is that everyone will learn the joys and rewards of self-discipline and how it can be used to make every area of life more satisfactory and fulfilling.

❧ I ❧

THE POWER OF SELF-DISCIPLINE

SELF-DISCIPLINE IS EXACTLY WHAT IT SAYS—THE ABILITY to discipline oneself. It is the ability to know what to do in situations and the fortitude to actually do what is correct in the situation. It is a habit that is vital to daily success. Truly successful people are usually highly disciplined people.

No one is born with the ability to *truly* self-discipline. Babies only care about being taken care of and having their needs met. As children grow older, their parents are in charge of their discipline—at least in the beginning. Parents make the rules, and children follow them because small children lack the thought processes needed to make good decisions on a regular basis. Small children only see the here-and-now, the immediate gratification. They do not know and do not care that a bigger, better reward might be in store for them if they wait patiently. They lack foresight. As children grow older, they begin to see the reasoning behind their parent's rules. They begin to make choices that mirror the choices their parents have made for them in the past. They show that they are learning to discipline themselves. At this point, the parents may begin to step back a little and to loosen the reins. They may allow the child a bit more freedom in making decisions, with the understanding that the parent is available if the choice turns out to be unfavorable. In this way, the child learns in the safety of the home and with the protection of the parents to make good choices and formulate good decisions. The child learns to self-discipline.

In a perfect world, this is the way children would be raised. Unfortunately, this is the real world and not a perfect one. The problem is not that parents do not care about their children—it is that many parents do not *know* how to teach the art of self-discipline to their children. Maybe the parents are not self-disciplined, maybe the parents feel the child will learn it eventually, or maybe the parents simply do not want to let go complete control over the child. For whatever reason, most children are not taught self-discipline as a way of life and reach adulthood with no clue of how to be in charge of themselves.

However, the good news is that self-discipline can be learned. While best learned while growing up, as a part of learning to be an adult, it is possible to learn as an adult and begin to practice self-discipline skills immediately. Moreover, by learning self-discipline in adulthood, the person has a total by-in to the idea. This is a personal choice. This is something that needs to be done in order to enjoy a better life. This does not mean that learning self-discipline as an adult will be easier or faster, but at least, the adult who makes the conscious choice to become more self-disciplined has a personal stake in its success.

Self-discipline is nothing more than managing one's own personal affairs. It is a way of behaving where people automatically choose to do what should be done, as opposed to what would more preferably be done. It is studying for a test instead of going to a party. It is washing dirty laundry on a regular basis so that clean clothes are always available. It is following a budget so that future financial goals can be realized. Self-discipline is that inner voice controlling outward actions. It is using willpower to become mentally tough enough to control one's actions by oneself.

Almost anything that a person does to focus on an end goal rather than immediate satisfaction is self-discipline. The underlying problem is that it is always much easier to follow the path of impulse. Impulse is fun. Impulse is now. Impulse allows for joining the group and having a fun night on the town instead of studying and doing laundry. Impulse is the exact opposite of self-discipline.

Granted impulse is much more fun than discipline. Impulse gives the opportunity to have fun and be with friends. Impulse means staying up late and sleeping in tomorrow. Impulse means spending the extra money on the desirable frivolous toy and not saving anything this week. But impulse will not finish homework, wash clothes, follow a schedule, or save money. Self-discipline is needed for those things. Does this mean that impulse has no place in a life ruled by self-discipline? Absolutely not! Impulsive action is an almost automatic action. A cake is meant to be eaten. Self-discipline should never be so rigid that people go through life acting like little robots with no feelings and no desires. Everyone wants a cake. Having self-discipline just means eating one slice of cake and not the whole cake.

Practicing self-discipline requires great self-knowledge. Think about that for a minute. How can anything be changed if all the facts are not known? Imagine walking into a kitchen and seeing a small child and a puddle of water. The first instinct would be to believe the child spilled something. But what if someone else spilled something and then left the puddle on the floor? What if the pipe under the sink is leaking? Without knowing all the facts there is no way to come to the correct conclusion. The path to self-discipline begins with knowing, and admitting the existence of, personal weaknesses. Everyone has those things they would rather not do. People would rather not admit to being imperfect, but all are and must be prepared to admit to imperfections to be able to begin the journey to self-discipline. The next step is to be prepared to move everyday temptations out of the way. This is usually easier said than done, but it must be done to properly begin along the path toward self-discipline. Once ready to begin, make sure to set clear, realistic goal and make a plan to achieve them. Do not be afraid to set several smaller goals as opposed to one large ultimate goal. Nothing worthwhile is ever reached in one straight path. There will be roadblocks and pitfalls along the way that will necessitate reworking the plan. So it may be better to start with smaller goals that will give a sense of accomplishment that will help ease travelling this path.

Keep the plan simple. Self-discipline does not need to be complicated. The idea of self-discipline itself is actually a very simple concept. The plan to get to self-discipline should not be overly complicated. The plan to reach self-discipline should be as simple as possible while encompassing all aspects needed to reach the goal. A complicated plan may be impossible to achieve and will probably lead to defeat—and giving up is not an option on the road to self-discipline.

Self-discipline is a powerful tool to possess. Self-discipline is a positive force in life. It does not mean giving up those things that make life satisfying; but rather using innate strength and creativity to achieve desired goals. With self-discipline, life is more enjoyable, and the little cheats that help make life enjoyable when people have the self-discipline to learn to enjoy these little cheats only occasionally. Again, it is not necessary to completely give up cake; just do not eat the whole thing!

Self-disciplined people do not deprive themselves, but they use focus to stay on track when goals conflict with one another. Let us imagine that friends want to have fun tonight with a pub crawl. Let us also imagine there is a huge chemistry test tomorrow. The self-disciplined person would stay home and study chemistry, thus giving better odds to getting a good grade and not worrying about the risk of oversleeping and missing the test altogether. The bars will still be there another time.

People who have a high level of self-discipline are more satisfied with themselves and how their life is going. Self-discipline allows for a better sense of self and a higher level of self-esteem. Life is not out of control. Life has meaning beyond today. Worthwhile goals are in sight in the future—and this works in a cycle. Creating goals and making a plan to achieve them leads to a higher sense of self-control. A higher sense of self control leads to more goal setting and plan making. The cycle just keeps going around.

Self-discipline allows for more time being able to do the things that will bring satisfaction and less of the things that provide no growth or satisfaction. Self-disciplined people set a goal and work toward it. Self-disciplined people are proactive, not reactive. This means they anticipate problems and work to prevent them, rather than trying to solve a problem when it occurs. Proactive people spend time every day wondering 'what if?'. *What if the car does not start tomorrow? What if the washing machine breaks down? What if the tree in the backyard falls into the house?* Proactive people imagine scenarios and decide on a plan of action before it is needed. If the plan is never needed then at least there is a plan in place. Reactive people, on the other hand, spend a lot of time doing things that are not producing a future goal. Reactive people react when the problem occurs. They have no preset plan in place. If the car does not start one morning then they scramble to find an alternate means of transportation for the day. The proactive person might give up eating lunch out every day in favor of brown-bagging lunch then saving that money for a down payment on a house. That is self-discipline. The reactive person will suddenly start scrambling trying to dig up down payment money for a house when the monthly rent increases yet again.

While missing restaurant lunches in order to save money for that future house might seem negative at the moment, it is positive in the long run. With a bit of sacrificing a future goal is achieved. Focusing on daily choices makes living more at the moment than looking toward the future. So while planning a daily brown-bag lunch might seem like an in-the-moment choice, it is really a part of a long term goal. Deciding on a different restaurant each day is truly in the moment—and when the goal is achieved, a tremendous sense of satisfaction replaces any feelings of deprivation that may have been lingering.

RAY VADEN

Boundaries are not scary things, but rather necessary limits to achieving a future goal. Boundaries are needed to achieve the level of self-control needed to become fully self-disciplined. Setting boundaries requires knowing exactly what the future goals are and how to follow a path to achieve them. This allows the self-disciplined person to understand themselves better than most people, to be much more comfortable in their own skin than most people. This also allows the self-disciplined person to know exactly what lengths they are capable of achieving in order to reach a goal.

Moreover, becoming self-disciplined will showcase who is a friend and who is not. True friends will assist in achieving goals. True friends will not try to block the hard work needed to become self-disciplined. By making the conscious decision to become self-disciplined, the sad truth of reality means that not everyone can stay around. But the self-disciplined person has the power to create the world as they want it to be.

Self-discipline takes an extreme amount of energy to achieve. It is not just choosing to be self-disciplined—it must be constantly worked at, and that takes energy. This will require good lifestyle practices. Eat healthily, sleep regularly, exercise when possible—all these activities will energize the body and mind and make working toward the goal of self-discipline more easily attainable.

HOW TO USE THIS BOOK

THIS BOOK IS INTENDED TO BE AN IN-DEPTH GUIDE TO developing self-discipline. It is not just a pleasant read to be read once and set on the coffee table to use for looks. This book is meant to be an in-depth guide toward knowing and implementing all the steps needed to achieve self-discipline.

Read through the book once, and then read through it again. The first read is merely to become familiar with what self-discipline really is. The second read should be slower and more in-depth to allow the reader time to process the tips and tricks included here and to imagine how these changes will fit into their current lifestyle. More importantly, this will allow time to begin to visualize these changes as a part of the everyday lifestyle and how the changes will fit.

Some of the ideas contained in this book will make more sense when they are actually used. Let's say that one goal is to save more money. Work out a plan to save—a personal plan. If cash is still the basis of most daily transactions, then put a dollar a day into a jar on the dresser. Take the spare pocket change and dump it in the jar every night. Many financial institutions offer ways to take money from the checking account, based on transactions, and transfer it to the savings account. A payroll deduction to a savings account might work. Whatever the method, the first most important step is to set the goal and the method that will be used to achieve the goal. Now, sit back and watch that money grow. Watch that jar on the dresser get a bit fuller every week. Watch how the amount in the savings account keeps increasing. This is how goals are achieved. It is not enough to want to save money. It is necessary to make the goal to save money as well as the plan to save money and then watch it grow.

Do not be afraid to try and fail. No one succeeds completely with the first attempt. Actually, that is a good thing. If self-discipline were that easy to achieve, then everyone would have it and possessing it would no longer be so special. Besides, trial and error is an important part of personal growth. The important thing is to begin, to try. Talking about beginning will not work. It is a good thing to spend some time considering this new journey, but the person who waits for some far off ideal moment will never begin. "Tomorrow," "someday," and "eventually" no longer have a spot in the vocabulary of the person who desires self-discipline. The time is *now*.

Use the ideas contained in this book and choose a goal. It does not—and should not—be a huge one. Start small. Smaller goals are much more manageable than large goals, and completing them is more certain. Completing a goal gives a marvelous sense of self satisfaction and helps drive one to further goal achievement. Make a plan to reach that goal. Start doing the tasks necessary to achieve that goal. Make the little sacrifices that have been identified as necessary to reach that goal. Give up the bad habits that need to go away. Embrace the new good habits that will lead to a better lifestyle and an increased ability to resist temptation. Trip and fall. Fail miserably. It will happen.

However, do not give up when it does. Get up, dust off the dirt, and start over. It may be necessary to rework the path to success at this point. Maybe the failure was due in part to a faulty plan. This also happens. No plan is inherently perfect. Every plan can and should be adjusted as needed.

K eep sight of the ultimate goal. Do whatever is needed to keep that goal fresh in the mind. Draw a picture and hang it on the refrigerator. Keep a detailed journal of daily events that will lead to the achievement of the goal. Tell family and friends about the goal. The more it is out front and visible, the harder it is to ignore—and by not keeping it a secret, the chances of failure are decreased. No one wants to fail in public!

B y using the ideas contained in this book and really putting effort into it, anyone can become more self-disciplined. It will not happen overnight—but with hard work and concentration, it will happen.

❦ 3 ❧

SELF-DISCIPLINE HABITS

SELF-DISCIPLINE IS A WORK-IN-PROGRESS AND A GOAL. THE goal is to become more self-disciplined. However, being self-disciplined is not something one achieves once and considers it done. Once self-discipline is achieved, it must be considered a lifestyle—it must be nurtured daily and constantly refreshed to stay relevant and useful. Self-discipline is a habit—a good habit to have to make life more worthwhile.

Self-discipline is the backbone of a successful person. Whether a person desires personal success, professional success, or both, self-discipline will lead them to their goal. It begins with a strong ability to control oneself with strict discipline. Thoughts are under control. Emotions are under control. Behavior is under control. This does not mean that thoughts never run wild and emotions never flow to the surface. It just means that they are never allowed to control the person. One might get a little misty eyed at the birthday card with the cute kittens on it, but one would not let this feeling take over the entire day. This is self-discipline. The person controls thoughts and emotions. Self-control becomes a habit—a new personal best friend.

A burning desire to achieve these goals will not be enough to achieve these goals. Strong knowledge of personal strengths and weaknesses combined with a good understanding of how to discipline oneself is the key to being successful. Good habits make the difference between failure and success.

Successful people know that discipline is the key that unlocks the door to future goal achievement. They use discipline daily to enable themselves to be able to achieve their dreams. They know how to use a strong foundation built on strong habits to enable them to be successful. They are fully aware that self-discipline will allow them to accomplish more in less time—making them a more valuable member of the team.

But where does this discipline come from? How does one person seem so at-ease with controlling their actions and behaviors while other people fail on a daily basis? How do some people live lives of total self-control, while other people never seem to know where their shoes are, much less where they are going? The answer is habit. Behavior is mostly driven by habit. If someone can control their habits, they can have strict control over their personal habits.

Moreover, developing good habits really is as simple as knowing where the shoes are. A self-disciplined person would have a dedicated space for shoes. When the shoes are removed from the feet they are placed in this dedicated space. The self-disciplined person is never almost late to work because they cannot find their shoes. If this sounds familiar, then try this little exercise. Pick a dedicated place for the shoes. It does not matter where; the closet, tucked under the bed, next to the night stand, wherever. The dedicated spot is a personal choice. Now, every night, make a conscious effort to put the shoes in the dedicated spot every time they are removed from the feet. One day, it will be apparent that this has become a habit—a good habit to have—because now, there is no more searching for the shoes on cold, dark mornings. While this exercise may seem quite simple, it is a prime example of setting a goal, making a plan to achieve that goal, and achieving that goal.

Good habits will allow a person to create a good plan for achieving future goals. Without good habits, self-discipline will never become a reality. But how are these habits developed? Why is it so difficult to overcome bad habits?

The problem is the pathways in our brains. Whenever a habit is begun, whether it is a good habit or a bad habit, the brain creates pathways that tell the body to act a certain way when certain things happen. A cigarette smoker will want to light up a cigarette when someone else does. Seeing the cigarette, smelling the cigarette, triggers the nerve pathways in the brain of a smoker to have their own cigarette. This is why cigarette smokers who are trying to quit are often encouraged to change some of their daily habits. Smoking is often tied to other activities. Beer drinkers who smoke will smoke more when drinking. Coffee drinkers who smoke will automatically light up while pouring that first morning cup. People who smoke on long car trips may be encouraged to chew gum instead. People who drink may need to stop frequenting the local bar. Coffee drinkers will need to find something to do with their hands instead of lighting a cigarette. The nerve pathways that the bad habit created can be broken. It will take time and hard work. But then NOT smoking becomes the new good habit.

Creating good habits from bad requires effort but it can be done. Good habits take time to build and bad habits take time to break. Start small, work hard and consider a few simple tricks that might help ease into the habit of fostering good habits.

Start by taking the time to be thankful for what is already present in life. Humans spend much more time than needed wanting bigger, better things. Once people learn to be happy with the things they already have and not waste time wanting things they do not have, they can begin to see what is really important in life and begin to make a plan to add to those things that are really meaningful.

Humans spend far too much time feeling useless emotions like guilt or anger. Negative emotions use way too much energy that is needed to focus on the good things in life. Letting go of negative emotions frees the mind, the heart, and the soul to be able to focus on the positive effects that building new habits will create. Learning how to let go of negative emotions is actually an excellent way to build self-discipline. It is a way of letting the world see the strength inside.

Daily meditation has a wonderful effect on the ability to become more self-disciplined. Meditation leads to a clear mind, a relaxed heart. It improves physical and mental health. A few minutes of meditation daily leads the body to sync up better with the mind. It is much easier to create good habits that will lead to self-discipline if the mind is relaxed and ready to receive good thoughts.

It is important to set specific goals by writing them down. Once a goal is committed to paper it becomes an active thing, something that can be seen. Goals that are kept in the mind do not have the same strength as goals that are written down. Goals in the mind can be forgotten or pushed aside. Goals written on paper are seen every time the paper is seen—and when they are written down, it is impossible to ignore them. They want attention. They want direction and planning. They want to be considered, cared for and loved. They want attention. Start small and work on them daily.

Remember to eat healthily and sleep well and regularly. The body cannot process new habits if it is undernourished. Good healthy food is crucial to giving the body enough energy to work on new and better habits. This is especially necessary when trying to break bad habits. Bad habits require extra energy to put aside. Sleep is especially important too. Most adults need between seven and nine hours of sleep every night. Play around with these numbers until the correct amount is determined, and then stick to that number. Make every attempt to go to bed at the same time each night and wake up at the same time each day. This is a good habit that will lead to self-discipline of personal habits. Of course, things happen, and sometime people fall off the schedule. But get back on it as soon as possible and do not regret one or two small slips. They happen.

Exercise is another good habit that must be settled into the daily routine. Regular exercise is important in keeping the body healthy. Usually, the word 'exercise' gives bad connotations to many people. But exercise does not need to be a negative thing. It does not mean running out to join the neighborhood gym or begin training for a marathon. Anything that gets the body moving is exercise. Go for a walk, jump rope, play with the kids in the front yard—anything, just get moving. Join a sports team. Remember how much fun baseball used to be. Rake leaves, clean out the garage, push the lawn mower around the yard. Regular movement releases stress and tensions and is another way to create a good habit.

Practice organization. Some people are naturally organized, and some people need to work very hard to be organized. If the latter group seems more familiar, do not try to become completely organized overnight. The organization will not happen but failure definitely will. Being well organized is a habit—and like any other good habit, it will take work to achieve. Begin by organizing one thing. Begin with a drawer. It is small and easy to organize. Have some boxes ready. When removing things from the drawer look at them closely and try to recall the last time they were used. If it has been more than six months then the item is not needed. Have some boxes ready while doing this. If the item is still in good condition it goes in the box to be donated. If the item is beyond usefulness then it goes into the box to go to the trash. Be firm! Do not hold onto something because it might get used. If it's a family heirloom and impossible to give up, put it in a box in the attic. When one drawer is clean, go to the next one. When all the drawers are organized move to the cabinets. As long as unnecessary items are not brought back into the house, then the house will remain clean and well-organized. Cleanliness will become a habit.

Time management is another goal that is necessary to embrace to build good habits and become self-disciplined. If there is no time management then time is the manager, and time is a very bad manager. Unmanaged time will slip away rapidly, leaving no time left in the day to do all the things that need to be done. Time management is nothing more than a plan to reach a goal of order and organization. An important part of time management is cleaning out the activities. Just like cleaning drawers of unused items, there are many unnecessary activities clogging up daily life. After the drawers and cabinets are cleaned and the house stays organized, one unneeded activity (constantly straightening the house) will be eliminated. It really is that simple.

Think of all the time that is actually wasted throughout the day engaging in unnecessary activities. How much time is wasted digging through a laundry basket looking for socks, when it would be so much quicker if the socks were in the drawer. How much time is wasted deciding what to cook for dinner when there is no set menu plan available to consult. How much time is wasted trying to find lost shoes? It all adds up.

No level of discipline will be successful without persistence. Temporary failure is not a reason to give up. Persistence is what keeps people going even through times of extreme failure. As far as progress goes, failure is an important part of life. Think of it not so much as doing something the wrong way but in finding yet another way that just did not work. In that instance, it is a learning opportunity and not a failure. This will also help lead toward greater self-discipline, by refusing to quit.

Habit and discipline go together hand-in-hand. Building a new habit is difficult in the very beginning because the body and the mind need to be taught a new way of thinking and working. But chasing good habits with persistence leads to greater self-discipline. The longer a habit is practiced, the more it becomes a part of the routine. It becomes easier. It becomes a habit, and no longer need to be practiced daily. It just naturally gets done—and once one new habit is set, it becomes much easier to add each successive one. If someone makes the decision to quit smoking, then not smoking is the new habit that will be cultivated. Once it has been persistently practiced long enough so that it is not so difficult anymore, then it is much easier to add healthy eating.

After all one good habit deserves another, right? With two new good habits in place, it just makes sense to add the habit of regular exercising. This is how new and better habits are formed and how habits build upon each other to create a lifestyle of self-discipline.

Self-discipline is nothing more than practicing a series of good habits until they become ingrained in the daily routine to the point where they are a part of life. As more bad habits are replaced with good habits, then the good ones take over and lead to a more orderly and organized life. As life becomes more organized, it becomes easier to manage—and now, it has become a life of self-discipline.

❧ 4 ❧

SELF-DISCIPLINE STRATEGIES
PART I – CREATING A PLAN AND
ACCEPTING REALITY

TO BE SUCCESSFUL AT DEVELOPING SELF-DISCIPLINE, ONE needs to make a plan. This plan will be different for everyone. No two plans will be alike. Each plan will be specific to the person who is making the plan. Everyone needs to develop a personal plan to be able to develop more self-control and, ultimately, more self-discipline.

Before creating a plan for self-discipline, it is necessary to accept life as it is now. Acceptance is the first most important step toward self-discipline. Acceptance means that life and reality as it exists now is truly accurate. Admit to what is. Acknowledge what is there. It is impossible to create change without knowing the full extent of the reality of now. Hence admit to the bad habits, the half-done items, and the failures left behind. Embrace them. Do this as kindly as possible. Do not use labels; they are self-defeating. A person is not fat; they need to lose weight. A person is not a slob; they need to get better at keeping the house clean. A person is not lazy; they need to become more organized at work using time-management strategies.

While this might seem like a simple thing to do, it is really very diffi-cult. Anyone who regularly has problems in one area of life probably has a serious flaw in that area. Continuous problems in one area point to the reality that all problems may be rooted in that area. It is not always an easy, obvious thing to see. It is usually an inability to see the true reality and accept it for what it really is.

Many people wonder why self-discipline is so dependent on acceptance of life as it really is now. This fact has its basis in the reality that makes the current situation one that needs change. Failing to correctly see the current situation means that honesty does not exist in this reality. Failing to fully see the current situation means that it cannot be fully accepted. Fully accepting the current situation is necessary for being able to create a plan for change. In anything that needs a plan, the first step is knowledge and acceptance of the current situation. If someone wanted to lose weight, for example, it would be necessary to know exactly what the current weight was, and to be able to accept that number as fact, before being able to make a weight loss goal and to create a plan to lose that weight.

Failing to accept the current reality means that improvement in this area is not really possible. Just like in the previous example, it is vital to know the current weight before the current weight can be changed —and that number must be accepted as it is. The number the scale gives is just the beginning. If it is more than expected then acknowledge it. The reality of now must be accepted before it can be changed. Now that it has been accepted and acknowledged, a plan for weight loss can be implemented. A goal can be set and hopefully achieved.

Working to increase self-discipline works the exact same way. It is vital to know where the level of self-discipline is now. Is it high and strong, or low and weak? What goals seem to be too difficult? Are any goals currently impossible to reach? When considering daily challenges, do not leave anything out. Think of all the things that cause struggles throughout the day.

Does the house need organizing? Is weight a problem? What addictions need to be faced and conquered? Are promises regularly kept? Is bathing a part of the regular daily routine? Is a regular sleep schedule observed seven days a week? Is regular exercise a priority? Are work hours focused or haphazard? Leave nothing out. No complaint is too small or insignificant, and that is just what these are—complaints of an unhappy life. When life lacks organization it cannot hope to be truly happy. When life lacks organization it lacks self-discipline.

It is common knowledge that muscles fall into separate groups and are best trained using different exercises. Just like muscles, the areas of self-discipline are very different and require alternate types of exercise to develop discipline. The best starting point is to identify an area where discipline is seriously lacking and develop a plan to train in this area first. Start slowly at first, building up to progressively harder goals as the training progresses.

Just as when building muscle, training self-discipline with ever increasing steps works well. Just remember to start with small goals and work up to large ones. Suppose the scale gave a number that was fifty pounds over what had been expected. After accepting that number as reality, a plan is made to lose those fifty pounds. It is not reasonable to expect those fifty extra pounds to be gone in a week or even a month, but it is not unreasonable to lose two pounds in a week. This would mean a weight loss of eight pounds in a typical four-week month. In six months and two weeks, the fifty pounds will be gone. This might sound like an extremely long time, but those pounds were not put on overnight and will not be lost overnight. Also, slow and steady progress is what makes habits. Good habits make self-discipline.

If it seems to be impossible to accept life as it is now, then the only things left are denial and ignorance. If the problem is ignorance then it will be impossible to ever know exactly how much discipline is lacking in everyday life. Unfortunately what is not known can hurt. There can be no hope of improvement without knowing exactly how much work needs to be done. If improvement is attempted without knowledge of reality then any failures will be blamed on the actual thing that needed change. If the problem is denial, then there is an incorrect view of reality—and just like being unable to accept the actual number on the scale, there will never be any progress toward goal completion because there is no discernable starting point.

Following the path to self-discipline will bring numerous rewards and benefits. Goals must be intentional. No one ever lost weight, found a better job, or organized the house without a plan to reach a goal. Progress does not just happen. It must be intentional. It must be reached on purpose. There must be a conscious effort to progress toward a given goal. No one accidentally became more self-disciplined. Goals must be reached progressively. This means that once a goal is successfully reached, work on the next goal is begun. Failure to continuously challenge the status of life will not gain self-discipline.

However, it is equally bad to try to push too hard when beginning this new journey. It is impossible to transform an entire way of life in one day. It just will not happen. Deciding to correct all bad habits at once in an attempt to develop instant self-control and instant self-discipline is a recipe for disaster—and failure just breeds more failure. If the goal is impossible to reach, and it is not reached, then it is taken as a sign that this whole process is impossible. Trying to set several new goals and expecting immediate perfection is a definite recipe for failure. Use whatever tiny bit of self-discipline already exists to build upon. The more self-discipline is practiced, the easier it becomes to build more. In the beginning, everything seems like an insurmountable challenge. As self-discipline grows the challenges become easier.

Never use other people's progress as a yardstick. Everyone develops at a unique pace. This is quite normal. This is not a race. This is a new lifestyle that requires hard work and dedication. No two people will face the same challenges, and no two people will develop at the same rate. Comparing the progress of two different people will only high-light deficiencies.

Building self-discipline requires creating good habits that will create pathways in the brain that will make the mind automatically default to good activity. Think of a little baby. Babies are not born knowing how to walk. Their little leg muscles just cannot hold them up. But babies are quite determined to be mobile. They see everyone around them standing on two feet and they know that they must also stand on two feet. So they find a piece of furniture, grab on, and try to pull themselves into a standing position. On the first tries, the baby falls back to the ground because its little legs are still not strong enough to support the body. But the baby is determined. So the baby keeps pulling on the chair until one day the baby is standing on wobbly legs while everyone rejoices. The baby's brain has created a pathway in the brain to that exact spot that controls standing in the baby's legs. Now that the baby has stood, that pathway is complete. It needs only to be used over and over so that the pathway, like the legs, will become stronger in time. A new habit is formed.

Once a habit is formed it must be built upon to create another habit. This is how the path to self-discipline is laid. Think again of the baby. Now that the baby is standing, the baby must learn to walk. It is not enough for the baby to just stand there because then the baby would not grow and develop properly and would never get across the room where the toys are kept. So something in the baby's mind tells it to put one little foot out in a step. The baby does that and falls down. There is no pathway in the brain for the act of walking—not yet, anyway. The baby will build one. This is using one habit to build upon to create another.

Never fall into the trap of looking at other people in a more favorable light. The misguided thinking that all other people are so much stronger is self-defeating. This exercise has no sense behind it. The only person whose progress is important is the person making the progress. Even identical twins do not develop at exactly the same rate. If they do not, then there is no sense expecting that everyone's progress will be exactly identical. Admit that this is where the starting point is, and this is a personal path to reach a personal goal.

Once reality has been accepted, once the starting point has been acknowledged, it is time to create the plan; the plan that will lead down the path to self-discipline. Begin with a clear vision of the goal.

Decide on the first thing that needs changing; set the first goal. An entire life of laziness and failure to succeed will not be corrected overnight. One goal must be achieved so that it can be used as a successful model and a building block for subsequent goals. Set the goal and formulate a plan for achieving the goal. Write it down on paper and look at it several times a day. Goals written down are more concrete than goals floating around in the mind.

Remove any temptations that will get in the way of achieving the goal. If weight loss is the ultimate goal, then clear the house of unhealthy foods. If stopping smoking is the ultimate goal, then toss the cigarettes in the trash. It may also be necessary to change parts of the daily routine. For example, if weight loss is the goal and the daily commute to work goes right past the best donut shop in town, a new way to work might be needed.

Keep the goal simple. Simple goals are easier to achieve than complicated ones. The goal 'to quit smoking' might be too difficult for someone who has smoked for decades and really depends on cigarettes in the daily routine. So a small goal would be best, to begin with. Begin by only smoking outside, never in the house. Even if it is in the middle of a blizzard or a monsoon, no smoking will be done in the house. Sometimes it just is not worth it to get up and go outside for a smoke. Then the first goal is achieved. There is no more smoking in the house. The next goal might be no more smoking in the car.

Smoking is a physical habit as well as a mental one. If quitting smoking is the goal then it will require getting past the physical cravings as well as creating a new pathway in the brain that leads to the idea of not smoking. Positive goals might include a fresher smell in the car or house, no more lingering smoke odor on the clothes. Perhaps when the urge to smoke hits it is replaced by a quick walk down the street or scrubbing the kitchen counter. This is how bad habits are replaced by good habits, and good habits build self-discipline.

Do not overlook willpower. Everyone knows that a stubborn person who just will not change their ways for anyone. That stubborn person possesses willpower. Willpower is just a nice word for stubborn. So be stubborn. Decide early what their goal will be and do not let anything get in the way of achieving that goal. Be stubborn about goal achievement. Do not take no for an answer. Do not change the goal no matter what happens. Being stubborn creates willpower that is vitally important to reach desired goals.

Create a plan, and then create a secondary plan. All good plans have a backup waiting in the wings for those awkward moments. If the ultimate goal is weight loss, then eating healthier will help achieve that goal. That is very easy to do at home where ultimate control over the menu exists. But since no one wants to be a hermit, what happens when the party invitation arrives? No happy human can resist a good party with friends and loved ones. But what about all that food? This is when the backup plan comes into effect. The plan to eat less is already in place. Now, the plan at the party might be to try one bite of everything offered and then to spend the remainder of the evening engaging in sparkling conversation with the other guests. This is the secondary plan. This will assist in keeping the original plan in place and allow the path to the goal to remain unbroken.

When setting the goal originally remember to allow for a treat when the goal is achieved. Humans work well on a system of rewards for good behavior. So chose a reward that fits the achievement of the goal. If smoking is no longer done in the house then buy some paint and refresh the walls. The house will look so much better and will smell marvelous. If the car is no longer smoked in then get it detailed; a fresh car smells amazing. If a weight loss goal is achieved, buy a new outfit, or at least one new wardrobe piece.

Moreover, accept that failure will happen occasionally. This does not mean to seek out failure. This means to accept failure when it happens —and it will. Humans are, well, human. They *will* fail. They will try hard, and they will sometimes fail. When failure happens, acknowledge its existence. Embrace the failure. Do not feel guilty or angry.

These emotions, while quite normal, only succeed in stalling any future progress that can occur once the path to the goal has been restored. Learn from failure. What happened? Why did it happen? How can this be avoided in the future? Once the failure is accepted and analyzed, it can be worked past. The path to the goal is still there. Maybe it needs a bit of reworking. Maybe a slight bend in the path is necessary. No matter what happens, getting back on the path is the first step in continuing on toward the achievement of the goal—and *that* is the first step toward self-discipline.

❦ 5 ❦

SELF-DISCIPLINE STRATEGIES PART 2 – REMOVE ROADBLOCKS AND PRACTICE PAIN

THE MOST BASIC COMMON TRAIT AMONG TRULY successful people is self-discipline. People who have a high level of self-discipline are traditionally more successful than people who are not self-disciplined simply because they have the inner strength to set a goal and do all that is needed to achieve it.

Think of a professional athlete. No good professional athlete allows themselves to get out of shape in the off season—or even in an off-week. Muscles must be constantly worked in order to keep up a certain level of strength and function. This means that pro athletes must have the self-discipline to commit to a training schedule of regular exercise even during the off season.

Self-discipline is a powerful personality trait to possess. It allows for a stronger sense of purpose and self-esteem. Self-discipline gives a feeling of accomplishment that may be otherwise lacking. The self-disciplined person is generally more open and honest with themselves because they know what they want out of life and have a plan in mind to achieve that goal. Self-discipline is the key to personal freedom.

But just as self-discipline can be nurtured and grown, it can also be destroyed quite easily. All paths lead somewhere. Once goals are set a path is created to enable access to that goal. But that path can be obliterated by debris. Life will set up roadblocks on a clear road whenever possible. Humans will also derail themselves by seeing a clear road and inventing roadblocks. Knowing what to look for will save time and trouble during the journey. Life happens. People get sick or injured. People get new jobs. People have new babies or move to a new house. Sometimes humans are their own worst enemy. They wonder what will happen if this, or that, or the other. They put road blocks in their own clear roads.

Remember willpower? Willpower is a vital tool in building self-discipline, but willpower can be overcome. Humans are weak, and donuts taste good. When people rely solely on willpower to reach goals, failure is surely following. Instead of planning to muscle the way through with sheer stubbornness, smart goal setters realize that temptation will happen and will likely not fall in the face of willpower alone. Instead, smart goal setters make a plan for the appearance of temptation and devise a way to stop it. The temptation is a roadblock that will hinder or completely stall progress if allowed.

This goes back to the idea of the party treats. The plan to avoid temptation is to sample one piece of each goodie and then spend the remainder of the night mixing and mingling. This is a plan to avoid temptation. The buffet at the party is a roadblock on the road to successful weight loss. A secondary plan for sampling the buffet and then walking away is a way of facing temptation head on—in essence, it is putting a roadblock in temptation's path instead of the other way around.

Another common roadblock—and one that many people fall prey to—is setting up hopes that are not realistic in everyday situations. People expect that once something is decided as a lifestyle change, then it becomes fact, and the world just does not work that way. A bad habit is a habit—and like any habit, it requires work to change to a better habit. People fail because the goals set are impossible to achieve in the way they were set. They may be too large, too soon, or too hard. Remember the pathways in the brain. A new habit must make a new pathway. Let's say the goal is to lose weight. Setting a goal of losing fifty pounds by next month is an impossible goal to achieve. It is too large, the deadline is too soon, and it would be too hard if not nearly impossible to lose that much weight in a few short weeks. It is far better to break the goal down into smaller, more easily attainable goals and not risk setting up false hopes that will never come true.

Self-discipline itself will not help anyone achieve an impossible goal. Neither will sheer willpower. There is a path to the goal. It is important to follow the path—one step at a time—until the goal is reached. It is vital to be aware that impossible goals are doomed to failure and not risk setting up impossible goals in the first place.

Another common roadblock in the path to the goal is stress. When people are experiencing extreme amounts of stress, the temptation is to ignore the path to the goal in favor of taking the easy path to self-indulgence. People who are under stress usually eat poorly or not at all, neglect exercise routines, and smoke like chimneys. They often become angry for no apparent reason and may stop taking care of cleaning their houses or persons. Attention to commitments often suffers as well, particularly the commitments made to reach specific goals.

Stress affects self-control. Self-discipline will not grow and develop if self-control does not exist. During times of stress, it is quite common to forget good intentions and revert back to bad habits. When this happens self-discipline will begin to deteriorate. This can be easily prevented by acknowledging the possibility that it might happen and preparing an alternate plan. Just as an alternate plan was made to avoid temptation at the party, have an alternate plan prepared to avoid falling victim to stress. Make an alternate plan to incorporate some sort of relaxation method into daily activity. Meditating, walking, listening to music, reading, enjoying a hot bath; the list is endless. The important thing is that this is used as a stress relieving activity to combat a rise in stress and it is seen as an enjoyable activity. It is usually not a good idea to try to beat stress by cleaning out the garage. Some activities will just bring their own level of stress. Look for the relaxing activities.

Self-discipline as a long-term goal depends on long-term work. A common problem people face when attempting to build good habits to develop self-discipline is not realizing how much work each goal will need. People want instant results. Someday is too far away. People tend to try to revamp their lives all at once. They will set several goals at the same time and expect them all to be easily attainable and to last forever and ever. The real truth is that even the people who are already highly self-disciplined need to work on new goals in small steps. It is even a good idea to take small, planned breaks periodically. A weight loss goal is a good thing. But it will be more easily attainable and seem less like a punishment if regular meals or even days are built in for a bit of cheating. People are human. Only the very strongest can resist temptation forever. With adding a meal to cheat periodically in a diet plan, it becomes less of a temptation and more of a secondary plan to avoid a roadblock, much like the party plan. It will be easier to stick to the diet plan knowing a treat is coming at the end of the week.

There are other ways to build in secondary plans to allow a bit of 'cheating' to avoid falling prey to large roadblocks. Work hard at work, but take regular time off to recharge and relax. Exercise well and often, but take days off to allow the body time to recover. Study hard, but allow for the occasional night out or spent relaxing in front of the television. Humans are not machines and cannot continue running indefinitely without either taking a break or breaking down—and without taking periodic breaks, the goal suddenly becomes a thing to be despised.

Time is another massive roadblock that can prevent the goal from ever being reached by preventing the path from ever being started. This is the type of time that is referred to in "I will begin working on my goal….." Once a goal is determined, then the start time must be determined. It should be as immediate as possible. Anytime someone says that goal achievement begins next week, at the beginning of the year, when things are going better, just understand that time will never come. Tomorrow never comes. So never intend to begin a new plan tomorrow unless it is named, as in a day of the week, such as "Tomorrow, Monday morning, I will….." Giving it a specific name gives it a specific start point. Not beginning immediately is just another way of saying goals do not matter.

Always keep in mind that self-discipline comes with pain. All humans feel pain at one time or another. Pain is a part of life. But choosing to feel pain in order to develop self-discipline may not seem like a very good idea. But it, too, is a necessary part of life. Remember that self-discipline involves doing what needs to be done as opposed to what would be more fun to do—and that in itself is painful. Achieving self-discipline means making sacrifices.

Remember that discipline is often used as a synonym for punishment. In a way it is true. Building self-discipline is painful and will often feel more like self-punishment. The self-discipline to follow a healthy eating plan may feel like punishment when there are fresh donuts in the break room at work. The self-discipline to stop smoking will seem like a punishment when everyone else is lighting up. The self-discipline to exercise regularly will definitely feel like punishment during the workout! The goal is easily visualized. Following the path to the goal is the hard part.

When working on self-discipline people must act as both the student and the teacher. Humans on a quest for greater self-discipline must be prepared to teach themselves the way to follow the path to the goal that will eventually lead to self-discipline—and that is where the underlying problem begins. While people usually love sharing knowledge and usually love teaching others what they know, they are often reluctant to learn from the very lessons they teach. Think of an overweight doctor. Common sense says that the doctor should be the first one with an acute awareness of the dangers of obesity. It is even reasonable to believe that the doctor is well equipped to teach patients how to monitor their own weight and adjust down as needed. Why, then, does the doctor not follow this same advice? Because it is much easier to tell someone else what to do than to do the same thing. Think of the teacher self as the adult and the pupil self as the child. It is not uncommon to hear adults tell children "Well, I'm an adult, so I can……." Simply being a grown up is not a free rein to do whatever seems like a good idea. But that is where a lack of self-discipline comes from.

The underlying problem here is that it is very difficult to teach oneself something one lacks knowledge of or the ability to perform. People can know what to do to become more self-disciplined, but the actual process of doing it may be difficult—and when humans fail at achieving self-discipline, are they to blame? No, it is usually some nameless outside force that caused the failure.

Think of the goal to lose weight. The outside forces that might cause a person to fail at this goal include holidays, getting morning coffee at the donut shop, snacks in the breakroom, and a marvelous sale on cookies at the grocery store. Any old excuse will do. If these outside forces did not exist then it would be easier to lose weight. But all of these things, and other excuses like them, are nothing more than the roadblocks that crop up in the path to self-discipline. They need accep-tance, acknowledgement, and an alternate plan to avoid them. Yes, this will cause pain. It is much easier to eat the donut than to ignore it. It might also be necessary to seek morning coffee at a place that does not sell wonderful tasting food. Perhaps morning coffee could be made at home.

When discipline causes pain it merely means the person is doing something they really do not want to do—but know they must do in order to achieve a greater goal. Staying true to a goal means giving up something pleasurable. Pleasure is not something given up lightly. But to hopefully avoid the future pain of failure the current pain of sacri-fice is necessary, even desirable. After all, pain can be a great motivator. The pain of giving up cookies in order to lose weight might be enough incentive to prevent future late-night cookie binges. So suffering pain now prevents greater pain later.

Discipline pain is not necessarily a physical pain but more of a commitment to a problem or issue. A commitment to lose weight will bring moments of pain. There will be a pain every time your favorite food is bypassed to allow consumption of something healthier. There will be a pain every time the scale does not show as much progress as was desired. There will be a pain, over and over, every time the goal is revisited and the realization dawns that the goal has not yet been reached.

People who are unwilling to suffer through the pain that comes with building self-discipline will later face the pain that comes from regretting the loss of a goal. Regret remains in the soul for a long time. It hangs over the heart, making life more difficult than necessary. The biggest difference between the pain brought by discipline and the pain caused by feelings of regret is that discipline pain will eventually end, while regret hangs around forever. There are ways to avoid the pain that comes with a lifetime of regret and leads to self-discipline through short-term suffering.

Find something to do that creates a great sense of passion within. Anything that creates internal passion means that it is something desirable, something wanted. It is so much easier to commit to feeling pain for a short time in order to reach a goal of something that is desired. This makes it much easier to stay on track with daily discipline. The goal must be believable and achievable.

Set priorities that are clearly defined. A goal can be interesting or it can be a commitment. It can be a noose around the neck or it can be a shining light at the end of the tunnel. Know when to commit to something and when to turn it away. Having a clearly defined plan to achieve a future goal is a constant reminder of the importance of sticking with the plan.

Once a goal has been chosen, feel free to share. Write it down on paper and tape it to the refrigerator. Tell the work buddy what is going on. Sharing the existence of a goal will often remove some of the pain associated with achieving the goal. When the path gets rough and starts climbing uphill it is wonderful if someone else knows the goal and can provide encouragement. This will help to remove a lot of the pain and replace it with encouragement and determination.

Make a mental picture of the goal. Do not spend too much time worrying about what it will take to achieve the goal. This is just a painful reminder of the pain that is waiting just around the next bend in the path. Instead, keep all focus on the goal. "I would love to eat a donut today, but I would be even happier fitting into a new swimsuit." Use what works. Even if the ultimate goal of weight loss is to be healthier, a little vanity never hurt anyone.

Choose a system of rewards and consequences. When goal setting for self-discipline, there is no outside force to put blame on if the plan fails. People choose to fall off the path, either intentionally or unintentionally. Since consequences are not pleasant, it is much better to set up a small series of rewards than to suffer future consequences that come with failure.

The pain that is naturally experienced while working toward a goal of self-discipline is a great strength builder. Self-discipline is wonderful for building muscles in the mind. Eventually, the mind will grow stronger and more resilient, and self-discipline will become much easier to maintain.

❧ 6 ❧

SELF-DISCIPLINE STRATEGIES
PART 3 – ACCEPT MISTAKES AND
REAP REWARDS

WHEN WORKING TOWARD SELF-DISCIPLINE, GOALS ARE made, and the path is determined. Resolutions are made and the journey begins. The way is not too difficult—progress is noticeable, and reaching the goal is becoming more of a reality every day. Then one day, it happens: a mistake. The pathway became momentarily too difficult to walk and falling off was the only option. The mighty has fallen—and now, lying beside the path and looking up at the goal that once seemed so close but is now even further away, the normal human might ask themselves, "What's next?"

People make mistakes. Things happen. Maybe the good intention of only eating one piece of cake at the birthday party was overridden by the fact that it was the best cake ever. Maybe the weeks of faithfully not smoking were ruined by one night at the bar. Maybe the weeks of running daily were interrupted by a major snow storm. Whatever happened, happened—and now, there is a mistake to deal with.

It is normal in life to make mistakes. The hard part is learning from the mistake. The person who can look at a mistake, accept it for what it is, and go on from there is probably someone who already has a great deal of self-discipline. The average person will look at a mistake, fall apart, and suffer regret. However, it is important to use the mistake as a learning experience in order to avoid repeating the mistake later.

There are steps anyone can take in order to recover from a mistake and get back on track. These are things anyone can do with any mistake, no matter how large or small it might be.

The first thing to do is to admit the mistake happened. Accept that people are human and flawed and mistakes will happen. Realize that it is not the end of the world, but a learning opportunity. This is often hard to do because humans do not like to admit to being less than perfect. Future progress will be delayed by failing to accept and own the mistake.

Next, realizing the difference between making a mistake and being a mistake is important. People are not mistakes. People do make mistakes. This distinction is crucial because making a mistake does not mean being worthless or meaningless. Making a mistake means being human.

Admitting to the mistake is important in another way. It is necessary to be able to understand exactly what went wrong. The why of the situation is very important. Things do not just happen, they happen for a reason. If the mistake in question involves losing sight of a goal and failing to follow the prescribed path to success, then why did this happen? What exactly caused it to happen? Was it one event or the accumulation of many small events?

Consider the goal to lose weight. The ultimate goal was set. The overall amount of weight to lose was decided. The smaller more manageable goals were decided upon. A system of periodic rewards was put into place. Then one day, a mistake was made. Was it the three pieces of birthday cake eaten at the party? Or did a disgruntled customer lead to a longer than normal workday that made the commute home later and longer in the pouring rain that led to the consumption of half a chocolate pie? Whether the mistake was caused by an isolated event or a series of events is important to know because it will assist in making a plan to avoid such mistakes in the future. If the event that caused the mistake was an isolated event, then a secondary plan should have already been in place to avoid such pitfalls. If one did not already exist, then now is the time to make one. The secondary plan can be as simple as eating something healthy before the party in order to avoid overeating, or by just deciding to exercise self-control and not eat more than one piece of cake.

If the mistake was caused by a series of events that led up to a minor catastrophe, then the secondary plan will be quite different. This plan would involve finding ways to avert disaster before one bad event piled up on top of another, then another, and so on. In the second scenario, it might have been a good idea to take a break after the disgruntled customer. Taking a moment to silently meditate, clear the mind and slow the breathing, might have prevented the series of disasters that followed and led to a binge eating event. It is important to know exactly what went wrong so it is not repeated.

Moreover, never forget there is something good in every mistake. Making a mistake allows a person to realize they are human. Making a mistake allows a new choice to be made—if needed. Perhaps the current path was not right in some way. Examine the path and decide if changes need to be made. Maybe the mistake happened because the path was not going in just the right way.

Sometimes life consists of one mistake after another. When this happens it is a definite sign that the path has too many flaws to be properly navigated for the time it will take to achieve the goal. This mistake might be the best thing ever—if used in the correct way.

So if the goals are wrong in some way, either too loose or too rigid, now is the time to restructure them. The path to the goal is never straight. It winds around obstacles, uphill, and downhill—until the goal is achieved. Perhaps this mistake happened because the goals were wrong in some way. Only the person who made the goals can determine that. Mistakes can be used as leverage to help renew a goal or change it as needed. A situation that is difficult, such as making a mistake, can help with future growth and goal setting—and the benefits that come from learning from a mistake are totally personally. They will always belong solely to the person who made the mistake.

Do not be afraid to use a mistake to its best advantage. This does not mean to constantly dwell on the mistake. Review the mistake as needed to get all possible learning from it. Then move on. Never let the mistake define the future. It was an event; do not make it a way of life. Learning from the mistake and moving on paves the way toward goal achievement. When that happens, it is time to reap the rewards of success.

Developing self-discipline often involves feeling pain for a short time in order to achieve a long term gain. This is sometimes difficult to do in a society where gratification is expected to be instant and satisfying. No matter what the goal is, finding the self-control from deep inside is often very difficult. But one of the main traits found with self-discipline is the strength to do without an instant pleasure in order to achieve a long term goal. This is especially true where the goal requires much effort.

Now that the first goals have been reached and the road to self-discipline is a familiar place, it is time to begin realizing the rewards—and the rewards of self-discipline are many.

The first reward of learning self-discipline is the fact that goals are now easier to set and to work toward. Personal priorities are more in line with the future desired goals. Having set priorities also leads to a better ability to focus on future goals. Decisions are easier to make without having to wade through bouts of confusion and uncertain ideas. Life is much more structured that it ever was before—and personal outlook on life improves drastically with every goal gained.

Developing self-control and self-discipline means that a person is well on the way to mastering control over themselves and their habits. It is easier to develop good habits to use to replace the former bad habits—

not to mention all the rewards that cultivating those good habits brings—and addictions and failures are less likely to take over because personal self-control has been mastered.

Emotions can bring a person down, both in mind and in the body—but having stronger self-control means fewer feelings of guilt over mistakes that have been made because fewer mistakes are being made. This is the joy of self-control. A person with self-control is able to resist the temptations that lead people into making mistakes that bring deep feelings of guilt and regret. Having the self-control to resist the temptation that would eventually lead to negative emotions is a reward in itself.

Living a life filled with self-control automatically leads to an elevated standard of life, at least emotionally. People with self-control and self-discipline know what they are worth and are not afraid to demand more of themselves in order to achieve ever increasing goals. The idea of receiving gratification immediately is no longer a viable option. Working toward a goal becomes a way of life.

Fulfillment comes to people with high self-discipline. These people have the ability to see a goal and develop a plan to work toward it, never wavering even in the face of adversity.

The biggest roadblock standing in the way of success has now been removed. The person creating the goals is usually the person's own worst enemy. But with experience in how to create the goals, stick to them, and reap the benefits of those goals—then the person has learned to correct flaws within themselves.

The level of self-sufficiency increases enormously. People who have demonstrated the ability to set goals and achieve them are much better at taking care of themselves. They have a vision of how life should be lived, driven by the goals they have already achieved and those they wish to achieve for themselves in the future. They are also much better at defining future goals and implementing a plan to reach those goals. These people have a clear view of their ultimate potential.

Moreover, having better self-control makes relationships with others even better. People with good self-control are seen as being more reliable and trustworthy. When people learn to work toward goals and learn to keep promises with themselves they are much better at meaning and keeping those promises made to others.

Self-discipline is a great time saver. People with self-discipline have control over their daily activities. Having discipline allows people to do things when they should be done, without procrastination. This in itself will save people a lot of time and energy. There is no longer a need to panic at the last minute, worrying over what will and will not get done. This allows for a calmer and collected lifestyle.

Now that life is well on the road to one filled with self-control and self-discipline, it is time to relax a bit before beginning work on the next goal.

7

FINAL THOUGHTS ON DEVELOPING SELF DISCIPLINE

SELF-DISCIPLINE IS THE ABILITY TO DEVELOP SELF-control over ones wants and desires and use them to develop a better person. As children, self-discipline is usually driven down our throats by parents and teachers alike. There is no way to escape the constant onslaught of being told that self-discipline will be needed to achieve any kind of success in life. Unfortunately, children usually just make faces and run away laughing.

As an adult, self-discipline and self-control is much more important than it was as a child. However, if this skill was not developed as a child, then it must be developed as an adult if any level of success in life is ever to be hoped for. It is quite true what all the parents and teachers said once upon a time. Self-discipline is the truth and the way.

So now comes the time for developing self-discipline by making small goals, achieving them, and working toward larger goals. Self-discipline is finding an important reason to achieve a goal and then making a serious commitment to work hard to achieve that goal. This may require completing a task or taking part in an activity that is not necessarily fun or pleasant at the time but that will bring future gains and rewards.

Developing self-discipline and self-control makes demands on a person. It is necessary to have a serious desire to do something better and to become a better person. It creates an internal drive inside a person to be a better person—and it helps create the motivation needed to work toward the desired goal.

Self-discipline gives people the ability to control inner desires in order to strengthen the resolve needed to achieve a goal. It is a way to keep impulses in check in order to allow time to focus on the achievement of a goal. If excess energy is not being used to chase desires that are not helpful in reaching any kind of meaningful goal, then that energy can be used for something more useful. Keeping impulses in line is another way to save excess energy and put that energy to good use— because achieving the desired goal requires focus and hard work.

Developing self-control and self-discipline depends on a constant daily focus on the methods required to consistently build everyday habits that will develop into the desired goal. Given enough time and energy, the outcome will be that the ideal goal is reached. This consists of taking baby steps. It will be necessary to practice consistent everyday actions that will form the basis of the path that will eventually lead to the desired goal.

Having self-discipline is not merely doing an activity regularly. It requires regulating daily habits to systematically remove the bad ones. It involves correcting the events that lead to the practice of bad habits, and it will mean regularly changing and adapting to changing events and conditions that may mean revamping life's circumstances and the pursuit of goals.

The key to growing a sense of self-discipline lies in being proactive about losing bad habits and not starting new bad habits. People are forced to train the mind to follow a new group of rules and to create new pathways to learn to follow these rules. More focus will be needed for daily tasks to ensure they align with the practice of new good habits and the loss of old bad habits.

There is great value in growing a good sense of self-control and, with it, self-discipline. Productivity in work, school, and life will be greatly improved. Self-confidence will soar with every passing day. A new level of self-discipline allows for a better sense of self-worth. It gives a greater feeling of control and a greater sense of being able to complete the necessary tasks at work and at home. It is easier to focus on tasks for longer periods of time. With this comes an elevated level of tolerance for other people and events in life. It will seem to take much less effort to be able to get more work finished in a shorter amount of time.

Self-discipline is a hard thing to master, but it gives its own set of rewards in a greater sense of self-worth and a greater ability to accomplish tasks—and achieving the desired goal can be its own best reward.

CONCLUSION

Thank you for making it through to the end of *Self-Discipline: Develop Daily Habits to Program Your Mind and Build Mental Toughness, Self-Confidence, and Willpower*! Let's hope it was informative and able to provide you with all of the tools you need to achieve your goals—whatever they may be.

The next step is to begin to use the steps contained in this book to revolutionize your life. Use these ideas to learn how to set goals, eliminate bad habits, get rid of negative thoughts and emotions, and just overall build a better lifestyle. People who have a higher level of self-control and self-confidence automatically perform better in school, at work, and just in life, in general. It is your time to shine.

Thus, use this book for what it was meant for—a self-help manual for developing a greater sense of self-control and self-confidence. Gaining a better level of self-confidence will require hard work and dedication. It will mean deciding what is important in life—what can stay and what must go. It may mean giving up some events that are fun— things that were once considered a vitally important part of life. It will certainly involve making great changes and experiencing many new things in life.

Building mental toughness is not as difficult as it sounds. It merely means using the growth of good habits to retrain the pathways in the brain to eliminate bad habits—and in the world of self-discipline, the word "willpower," also known as personal stubbornness, is a good thing.

So please, use this book and the tips and trick contained inside to better your own life. Read the examples so that you will fully understand the point that is being made. Make notes if you find that helps you to better understand and remember. Read the book, and then read it again more slowly. Study it closely. The advice in this book is meant to give you a chance to make your life much more fulfilling by increasing your personal level of self-control and self-confidence.

Realize that these changes will not happen overnight. Change for the better always takes time. It is necessary to eliminate the bad habits while working to cultivate the good habits one wants to pursue. This might mean changing such habits as for where you drive, where you eat, and when and where you decide to go out for a fun evening—but know that at the end, when self-confidence is at an all-time high, that the journey was well worth it.

Finally, if you found this book useful in any way, a review on Amazon is always appreciated!

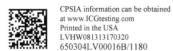

CPSIA information can be obtained
at www.ICGtesting.com
Printed in the USA
LVHW081313170320
650304LV00016B/1180